The Beginner's COMPUTER Dictionary

Other Avon Camelot Books by
Elizabeth S. Wall

THE COMPUTER ALPHABET BOOK

ELIZABETH S. WALL grew up in New York City and teaches computer programming to 5th graders. She now lives in Florida with her husband Alexander.

ALEXANDER C. WALL grew up in Philadelphia, PA. He is an electrical engineer. He has developed, among other things, robots, and pretzel-twisting machines.

MICHAEL MARKS is a sculptor and illustrator and has contributed to *Sesame Street* and *The Electric Company* magazines. He also teaches a studio workshop for children at the Los Angeles County Museum.

The Beginner's COMPUTER Dictionary

Elizabeth S. Wall
and Alexander C. Wall
Illustrated by Michael Marks

3rd grade reading level has been determined by using the Fry Readability Scale.

THE BEGINNER'S COMPUTER DICTIONARY is an original publication of Avon Books. This work has never before appeared in book form.

AVON BOOKS
A division of
The Hearst Corporation
1790 Broadway
New York, New York 10019

Text illustrations by Michael Marks

Text design by Sheldon Winicour
Published by arrangement with the authors
Library of Congress Catalog Card Number: 84-45080
ISBN: 0-380-87114-9

Library of Congress Cataloging in Publication Data

Wall, Elizabeth S., 1924-
The beginner's computer dictionary.

Summary: An alphabetically-arranged list of computer terms with definitions.
1. Computers—Dictionaries, Juvenile.
[1. Computers—Dictionaries] I. Wall, Alexander C.
II. Title.
QA76.15.W284 1984 001.64'03'21 84-45080
ISBN 0-380-87114-9

First Camelot Printing, June, 1984

Printed in the U.S.A.

OP 10 9 8 7 6 5 4 3 2

The Beginner's COMPUTER Dictionary

A

ABACUS—The world's oldest calculating machine is a frame with wires or rods on which beads are moved up and down to add and subtract.

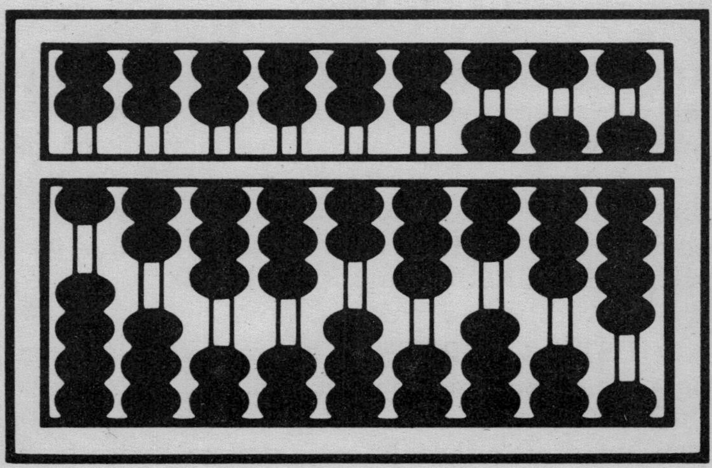

ABS—Short for absolute, a word in BASIC that means "change to absolute value" (see ABSOLUTE VALUE).

ABSOLUTE VALUE—To change negative numbers to positive and leave positive numbers unchanged (see ABS).

AC—Short for alternating current.

ACCESS TIME—The length of time taken between requesting data from the computer and receiving the data (see DATA).

ACCESSORY—A piece of hardware added to the computer. For example, a printer, disk drive, or modem are accessories which help the computer do more jobs (see HARDWARE).

ACCUMULATOR—The "king" of the registers in the microprocessor. The accumulator is the place where the computer puts data as it moves from one place to another. For example, the accumulator is like a bucket which holds data until it's ready to be moved to another part of the computer (see MICROPROCESSOR and REGISTER).

ACOUSTIC COUPLER—A box connected to a computer which holds a telephone hand set. The acoustic coupler listens to the telephone message and changes it into a code the computer can understand.

If you put your ear close to the acoustic coupler, you'll hear the message beeps.

ACRONYM—A word made from the first letters of a phrase. For example, the acronym ROM is short for "read only memory."

A/D (A to D)—Short for analog to digital. A/D describes a circuit which changes an analog signal to a digital signal. For example, when you move the handle on a paddle, your hand motion is analog and the A/D circuit in the paddle changes your hand signal to a digital signal which the computer can understand (see ANALOG, CIRCUIT, and DIGITAL).

ADAPTER—A connector which allows two different-size parts to be put together. For example, you may have used an adapter at home or school to connect a three-prong plug to a two-prong outlet.

ADDRESS—The number of a place in a computer's memory where data is stored. Just like your house, each place in memory has an address number (see DATA).

ALGORITHM—A step-by-step way to solve a problem. For example, the algorithm to find how many quarters there are in two dollars is:

Step 1. Take the number of dollars (2).
Step 2. Multiply 2 by the number of quarters in one dollar (4).
The answer is 8 quarters.

ALPHANUMERIC—Any letter, numeral or special sign that has an ASCII code is an alphanumeric character (see ASCII).

AMPERSAND (&)—A sign on the computer keyboard that means "and."

ANALOG—A way of describing something without numbers. For example, hot, warm, chilly, or freezing is an analog description of weather temperature. Computers cannot read analog data. All data given to a computer must be digital. For example, the same weather data given to a computer must be the digits 95, 80, 50, and 25.

APOSTROPHE (')—An English language sign that replaces letters missing from a word.

ARRAY—A list of letters or numerals in rows and columns. For example, football and baseball scoreboards that show teams and scores are arrays.

ARITHMETIC UNIT—The part of the computer that does all the math in a problem. It can add, subtract, multiply, and divide in a flash.

ARROWS—Signs on the computer keyboard which move the flashing cursor forward, backward, up, or down (see CURSOR).

ASCII—Short for American Standard Code for Information Interchange. ASCII code is used by computers in place of English letters, signs, and numbers. Every letter, sign, and number has an ASCII code in decimal, hexadecimal, and binary. For example:

	Decimal	*Hex*	*Binary*
A	193	C1	1000001
B	194	C2	1000010
+	171	AB	0101011
$	164	A4	0100100
1	177	B1	0110001
2	178	B2	0110010

ASSEMBLER—A computer program on disk or in ROM which changes assembly language into machine language (see ASSEMBLY LANGUAGE, ROM, MACHINE LANGUAGE).

ASSEMBLY LANGUAGE—The name of a computer language. Each computer has its own special assembly language. Each line in an assembly language program starts with a short code word of 3 or 4 letters. For example:

LDA means **L**oa**D A**ccumulator
TXA means **T**ransfer data in register **X** to **A**ccumulator

ASTERISK (*)—A sign on the keyboard which looks like a star. In BASIC, it tells the computer to multiply (see BASIC).

B

BACKSPACE—To move the cursor back one space. The backspace key on a computer keyboard has "BACK SPACE" or "BSP" on it. It usually erases when it moves back. Some computers use a back arrow (←) for backspace (see CURSOR).

BACKUP—Make an extra copy of a disk or a cassette.

BAR CODE—Groups of thin and thick printed bars that can be read with a wand or a light beam to send data to a computer. Most supermarket grocery products have bar codes printed on them.

Bar Code

BASIC—Short for **B**eginner's **A**ll-purpose **S**ymbolic **I**nstruction **C**ode. BASIC is the name of one computer language used to write programs. Most home and school computers know BASIC. It uses many English words like END, GOTO, IF. . .THEN, PRINT, and RUN. Each program line in BASIC must begin with a number (see PROGRAM).

Here's a short BASIC program. Do you know what it tells the computer to do?

```
10 PRINT "HELLO"
20 END
```

BAUD—Speed of sending data over a telephone line. One baud equals about one bit per second (see BIT).

BELL—A computer word for a sound signal—usually a beep from its inside speaker. Most computers will beep the speaker when you press the CTRL key and the G key together.

BINARY—Means 2. Binary numerals are 1 and 0. The computer only understands these two numerals. You can use English words and numbers you know to send a message into the computer, but inside, the interpreter or compiler program changes each letter and number in your message to the ASCII binary code of zeros and ones (see ASCII, COMPILER, and INTERPRETER).

Here's what some of our numbers and letters look like written in ASCII binary code:

0 = 0110000   A = 1000001
1 = 0110001   B = 1000010
2 = 0110010   C = 1000011

BIT—Short for the two words **B**inary dig**IT.** A bit is 0 or 1. All letters and numbers are coded by the interpreter or compiler program inside the computer to bits (see COMPILER, INTERPRETER).

For example:
Number 5 is coded to the 7 bits 0110101
Letter A is coded to the 7 bits 1000001

BOOT—To tell the computer to use the "bootstrap" program to get started. Some computers boot when you turn on the power. Others boot after you turn on the power and type a special command such as PR#6 (see BOOTSTRAP).

BOOTSTRAP—Short for "bootstrap program." A special program in ROM which lets the computer start itself (see PROGRAM).

BRANCH—To leave one path in a computer program and take another path (see PROGRAM).

BREAK—To stop a program. Some computers have a "BRK" or break key which, when pressed, stops the computer while running a program. Others use the keys CTRL and C to stop a running program (see PROGRAM).

BUG—A mistake or trouble in a computer program or equipment. A bug in a program gives the wrong answer or may even make the computer stop running the program. You must find the bug and correct it before the computer can go on with its job.

BUFFER—A small memory in the computer used to store data for a short time.

BUS—A special set of wires inside a computer. Electrical signals pass from one part of the computer to another over a bus.

BYTE—A string of 8 binary bits, or 1's and 0's. For example, 01000001 is a byte.

C

CABLE—A bundle or flat band of wires used to connect different parts of the computer system. These parts are usually the computer, monitor, disc drive, and printer (see COMPUTER, MONITOR, DISK DRIVE, and PRINTER).

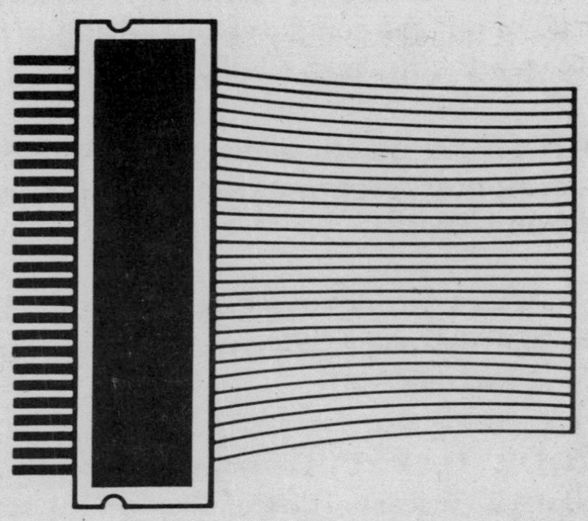

CAI—Short for **C**omputer **A**ssisted **I**nstruction. You use CAI programs on your school computer. They're math, language, or social studies programs which ask you questions and tell you right away if your answers are right or wrong (see PROGRAM).

CALCULATOR—A small machine that you can usually hold in your hand to do arithmetic fast and accurately.

CALL—A BASIC word followed by an address number. It tells the computer to run a machine language program which it finds at that address (see ADDRESS, MACHINE LANGUAGE, and PROGRAM).

For example, CALL 64477 will beep the speaker on an APPLE computer.

CARET ( )—A math sign on the keyboard. It's used in BASIC to tell the computer to multiply a number by itself (see BASIC and KEYBOARD).

CASSETTE—A plastic box which holds tape on which computer programs are stored (see PROGRAMS and TAPE).

CATALOG—A BASIC word that tells the computer to show the list of programs stored on a disk (see DISK and PROGRAM).

CATHODE RAY TUBE—An electronic picture tube, like a TV screen. It's the place on the computer where messages are shown. CRT is a short name for cathode ray tube (see VACUUM TUBE).

CENTRAL PROCESSING UNIT—The computer's "brain," which follows the instructions given in a program. It tells the other parts of the computer what to do. CPU is its short name (see CPU and PROGRAM).

CHARACTER—A letter, number, or sign on a keyboard. In BASIC, the short form looks like this: "CHR." Every character has an ASCII code (see ASCII).

CHIP—Short for silicon chip, a tiny part used in making computers. Chips are used in computers for such things as memories, CPUs, or arithmetic units (see ARITHMETIC UNIT, CPU, and MEMORY).

CHR—Short for "character" and usually used in BASIC with this sign ($) called string.

For example, PRINT CHR$(193) tells the computer to change the character string 193 into its ASCII code letter, which is A (see ASCII).

CIRCUIT—A set of electrical paths.

CLEAR—A key on some computer keyboards. It acts like magic and erases everything from the screen.

CLOAD—A BASIC word that tells the computer to get a program from a tape cassette and put it in memory.

CLR—Short for CLEAR (see CLEAR).

COBOL—Short for **CO**mmon **B**usiness **O**riented **L**anguage, the name of a computer language used to write programs for businesses (see LANGUAGE, PROGRAM).

CODE—Letting numbers or letters mean something different from their regular meaning (see ASCII).

COLON (:)—The sign on a keyboard. In BASIC, it lets a user send two or three commands to the computer before pressing RETURN or ENTER.

For example: HOME:NEW tells the computer to erase the screen and erase everything in its memory (see RETURN and ENTER).

COLOR—A word in BASIC, followed by an equals sign (=) and a color code number, tells the computer what color to show on the screen. Some computers can draw in 15 colors.

For example: COLOR=3 tells the computer to draw the next lines in purple.

COMMA (,)—A punctuation sign used in a BASIC PRINT statement. It tells the computer to jump several spaces and then print the next word.

For example, the program:

```
10 PRINT 1,2,3
RUN
```

The computer would print

```
1        2        3
```

COMMAND—An order telling a computer to do something.

COMPILER—A special program which changes a user's program written in another language, such as PASCAL, into machine language. A compiler changes the whole program before running it. The compiler program may be on a disk or on a ROM chip (see PROGRAM, MACHINE LANGUAGE, LANGUAGE, ROM).

COMPUTER—A machine with a memory that accepts data, works on a problem, and prints out the answer. It can do arithmetic, read, write, count, and remember faster and better than anybody (see DATA, MEMORY).

CONSTANT—A number that never changes. It's the opposite of variable (see VARIABLE).

CONTROL—A key on the computer keyboard which, when pressed with another key, tells the computer to look at its control chart in memory for a special job. CONTROL does not print anything on the screen. The short form looks like this: CTRL. For example, CONTROL C stops a running program (see KEYBOARD, MEMORY).

CONT—Short for continue. This BASIC word tells the computer to restart a program which has been stopped by BRK or CONTROL C (see BRK, CONTROL, PROGRAM).

CPU—Short for Central Processing Unit (see CENTRAL PROCESSING UNIT).

CRT—Short for Cathode Ray Tube, a picture tube, or computer screen (see CATHODE RAY TUBE).

CSAVE—A BASIC word that tells the computer to take a program from its memory and save it on the tape cassette (see MEMORY, PROGRAM, TAPE).

CTRL—Short for control (see CONTROL).

CURSOR—A flashing mark on the computer's screen which shows where the next character will print.

D

DATA—(1) The digits or numbers, letters, and signs the computer needs. For example, PRINT "JULY 4, 1776," is input data that tells the computer to output the date. It has digits, letters, and signs (see DIGITS, INPUT, OUTPUT, SIGNS);

(2) a word in BASIC that tells the computer to store a list of words.

DATA BASE—A collection of data usually stored on disks or tape.

For example, if all the words in this dictionary were stored on a disk, that would be a computer dictionary data base (see DISK, TAPE)

DATA PROCESSING—What the computer does with data stored on the disk.

For example, if you asked the computer to list all the words beginning with "D" in the dictionary data base, the computer would process the words and print out all the words beginning with the letter "D" (see DATA BASE).

DEBUG—To find and correct a mistake in a program or fix the computer if it's broken (see BUG, PROGRAM).

DECIMAL—A number system using 10 symbols or digits. For example, we use the decimal system every day.

DECISION—The name of a special box in a flowchart where the computer takes one of two paths, depending on the answer to the question (see FLOWCHART).

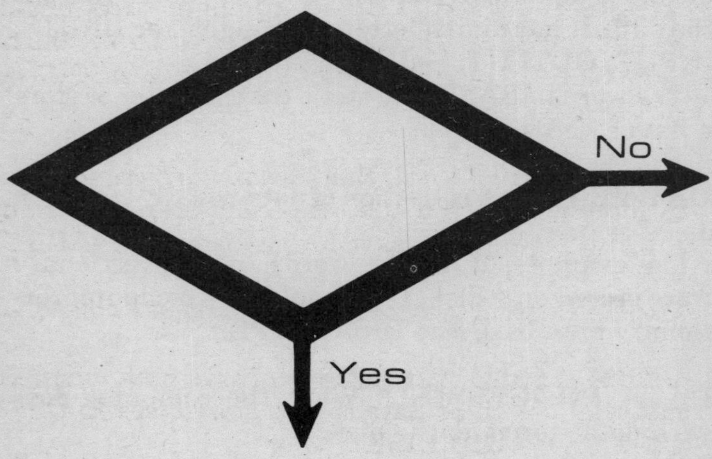

DECODE—To discover the meaning of something written in code (see CODE).

DELETE—Take out or erase. On some computer keyboards a delete key looks like "DEL."

DIGIT—A single numeral. For example, 0, 6, or 9 are single-digit numerals and 15 is a two-digit numeral.

DIGITAL—A way of describing something entirely with numbers. All data must be given to the computer using digits.

For example, to tell the computer to show the color red, you type COLOR=4. The number 4 stands for red. DIGITAL is the opposite of ANALOG (see ANALOG).

DIGITAL COMPUTER—A computer that understands only binary coded digits. For example, the binary code for the digit 9 is 01101001 in ASCII (see ASCII).

DIM—A BASIC word, short for dimension, followed by numbers, which tells the computer how many rows and columns to save for an array (see ARRAY).

DISC—Another way of spelling disk (see DISK).

DISK—A round, flat surface covered with magnetic material on which data can be stored (see FLOPPY DISK and HARD DISK).

DISK DRIVE—The part of the computer which runs the disk.

DISKETTE—A small disk.

DISPLAY—To show something. For example, the computer displays a program or picture on its screen or cathode ray tube (see CATHODE RAY TUBE, PROGRAM, SCREEN).

DOCUMENTATION—The written description of hardware or software (see HARDWARE, SOFTWARE).

DOLLAR SIGN ($)—The sign on a computer keyboard which can have several special meanings. One meaning, in BASIC, with a letter in front of $ is a string or row of things. For example, A$ = "ABCD" means that each time the computer sees A$ in a program, it uses ABCD. Another meaning, when $ precedes a digit, is that the following digits are hexadecimal. For example, $1A is the hexadecimal name for 26 (see BASIC, DIGIT, HEXADECIMAL, PROGRAM, STRING).

DOS—Short for Disk Operating System. It is a program which tells the computer and the disk drive how to work together (see DISK DRIVE, PROGRAM).

DOT MATRIX—Sets of small dots used in fast printers to print characters on paper.

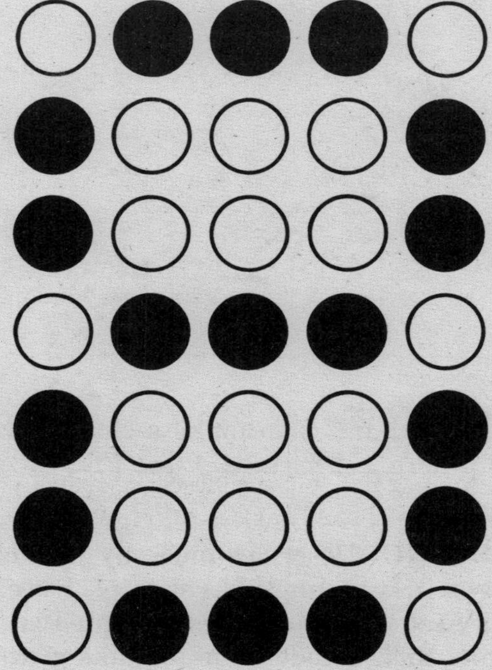

DRAW—A BASIC word followed by numbers which tells the computer to get a shape from memory and draw it on the screen (see MEMORY).

DRIVE—Short for disk drive.

DUMP—To copy all or part of the computer's memory from one place to another (see MEMORY).

E

EDIT—To read and then make a change or correction in a program if necessary (see PROGRAM).

ELECTRONIC—Describes one way of controlling electricity with vacuum tubes or chips. For example, in most TV sets, vacuum tubes and chips catch radio signals and then decode them to make pictures and sound (see VACUUM TUBE and CHIP).

ENIAC—Short for Electronic Numerical Integrator Calculator, the first electronic computer. It used only vacuum tubes to control electricity because chips had not yet been invented (see ELECTRONIC and VACUUM TUBES).

END—The word in BASIC that tells the computer to stop.

ENTER—To put data into the computer. Some computers have a key named ENTER and when it's pressed, it tells the computer it's okay to take this data into the computer.

EQUALS (=)—A keyboard sign which tells the computer "from now on, use what's on the right of = instead of what's on the left." For example, A=4 means "from now on use 4 instead of A whenever you see A."

ERASE—To remove data from memory (see MEMORY).

ERROR or ERR—The word a computer uses to tell you that something is wrong.

ESCAPE—Some computers have a key named ESCAPE or ESC. When pressed, it does not print anything. Instead, it sends a code to the computer that tells it to do a special job (see CODE).

EXCLAMATION MARK (!)—A sign on the keyboard, used most often in programs as a special code (see CODE, KEYBOARD, PROGRAM).

EXTERNAL MEMORY—A place for storing data outside the computer. For example, a disk or tape is an external memory for computer programs (see DISK, MEMORY, PROGRAM, TAPE).

F

FILE—A collection of data which belongs together. Every file must have a name so the computer can find it. One example of a file is a program (see DATA and PROGRAM).

FIRMWARE—Data or a program stored on a chip inside the computer (see CHIP, DATA, PROGRAM).

FLOPPY DISK—A soft, round record on which data and messages for the computer are stored. The disk comes inside a paper or plastic cover and is *always* used inside its cover.

FLOWCHART—A drawing of all the instructions in a program. Each instruction is shown in a box. The boxes are connected by lines to show what happens in the program from beginning to end. For example, this flowchart shows what steps to take to put three letters in ABC order (see INSTRUCTION, PROGRAM).

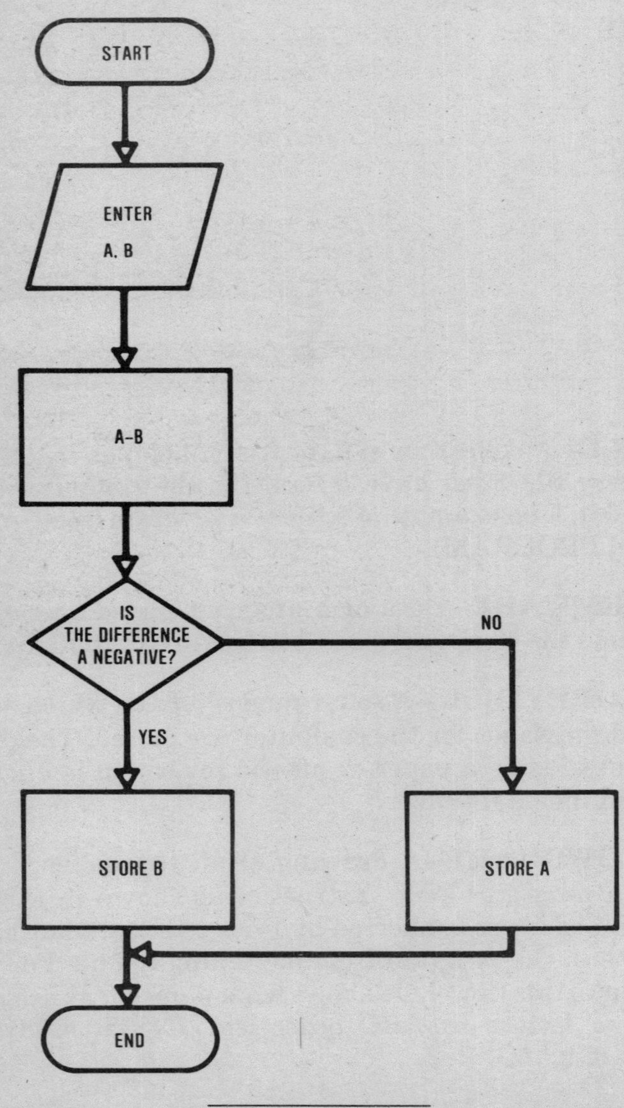
START
ENTER
A, B
A–B
IS
THE DIFFERENCE
A NEGATIVE?
NO
YES
STORE B
STORE A
END

FOR—A word in BASIC used with the BASIC word NEXT. These two words together in a program start the computer counting how many times to go around a loop (see LOOP, PROGRAM).

For example :

```
10 FOR X= 1 to 5
20 PRINT X
30 NEXT X
```

Makes the computer print

```
1
2
3
4
5
```

FORTRAN—Short for **FOR**mula **TRAN**slation, a computer language used by scientists and engineers (see LANGUAGE).

G

GIGO—Short for garbage in, garbage out. If computer input is wrong, computer output will be wrong (see INPUT, OUTPUT).

GLITCH—A surprise electrical jiggle that messes up what the computer is doing at that moment.

GOSUB—Short for "go to subroutine." GOSUB is a word in BASIC followed by a line number which tells the computer to go to a little program. The last instruction in the little program must be the BASIC word RETURN to tell the computer to go back where it started (see INSTRUCTION, PROGRAM, RETURN).

GOTO—A word in BASIC always followed by a line number. This tells the computer to go to that line number for its next instruction (see INSTRUCTION, LINE NUMBER).

GR—Short for GRAPHICS, GR tells the computer to get ready to draw pictures instead of writing words (see TEXT).

GREATER THAN (>)—A relational sign which asks the computer to find out if whatever is in front of the sign is bigger than what's in back of the sign.

H

HANG—Means the computer is lost in a program loop and won't pay attention to any key except RESET (see LOOP, PROGRAM, RESET).

HARD COPY—Computer output printed on paper. Only computers with printers can make hard copy (see OUTPUT).

HARD DISK—A hard, smooth, round record on which data for the computer are stored. The disk is locked inside the disk drive and cannot be touched. It stores much more data than a floppy disk (see DATA, FLOPPY DISK).

HARDWARE—Any computer parts you can see and touch, such as keyboard, disk drive, and video screen (see KEYBOARD, DISK DRIVE, VIDEO SCREEN).

HELLO—The name of a program often used to initialize a disk (see DISK, INITIALIZE, PROGRAM).

HEX—Short for hexadecimal (see HEXADECIMAL).

HEXADECIMAL—The number system that uses 16 instead of 10 for its base. Assembly language programs use a hex number system instead of decimal (see ASSEMBLY, LANGUAGE, PROGRAM).

For each HEX number there is a decimal number. For example:

Decimal	*Hex*
0	0
6	6
9	9
10	A
15	F
16	10
20	14
30	1E
100	64
256	100

HLIN—A word in BASIC that tells the computer to draw a line across the screen from left to right. For example:

```
10    HLIN 10,29 at 5
```

HOME—A word in BASIC which tells the computer to clear the screen and send the cursor to the upper left-hand corner (see CURSOR).

I

IC—Short for integrated circuit. Many ICs are used to make a computer (see INTEGRATED CIRCUIT).

IF—A word in BASIC used to tell the computer that a relational sign is coming. For example:

```
10 IF A     5 THEN PRINT A
```

If A is 6 or more, the computer will print the number. If A is 5 or less, the computer will print nothing (see RELATIONAL SIGNS).

INFORMATION—A collection of data that has meaning. July 4, 1776, is a collection of data that has definite meaning (see DATA).

INFORMATION RETRIEVAL—The process a computer uses to find data in its memory and bring it back to the user (see DATA, INFORMATION, MEMORY, USER).

INIT—Short for initialize. INIT is a command that tells the computer to get a disk ready for input (see DISK, INPUT).

INITIALIZE—Making a disk ready for input. New, unused disks must be initialized before they can accept input (see DISK, INIT, INPUT).

INPUT—Data put into the computer (see DATA).

INSTRUCTION—A single program step (see PROGRAM).

INT—A word in BASIC, short for integer, which tells the computer to use only whole numbers.

INTEGER—A whole number.

INTEGRATED CIRCUIT (IC)—A small computer part with groups of electrical circuits connected together. The IC circuit is made on a silicon chip and covered with plastic for protection. Computer parts such as RAMs, memories, and CPUs are integrated circuits (see CIRCUIT, CHIP, SILICON, RAM, MEMORY, CPU).

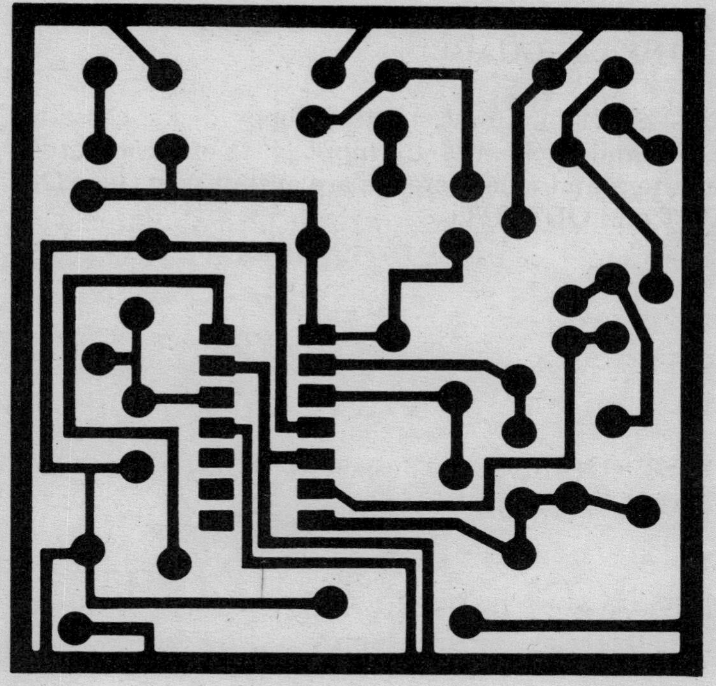

INTERFACE—A computer part needed to send data back and forth between pieces of hardware (see DATA, HARDWARE). For example, an interface is used to send data between the computer and the printer.

INTERPRETER—A computer program which changes programs written in one language, such as BASIC, into machine language. An interpreter changes the program one line at a time as the program is run (see PROGRAM, LANGUAGE, MACHINE LANGUAGE).

I/O—Short for input/output. Floppy disks, cassette tapes and keyboards are input parts of a computer. Printers and video screens are output parts (see INPUT and OUTPUT).

J

JACK—The place where a plug is inserted.

JACKET—The plastic cover for a floppy disk (see FLOPPY DISK).

JOYSTICK—A small stick mounted on a box and connected by a cable to the computer. When you move the stick with your hand, it sends signals through the cable to the computer. Another name for joystick is paddle (see A/D).

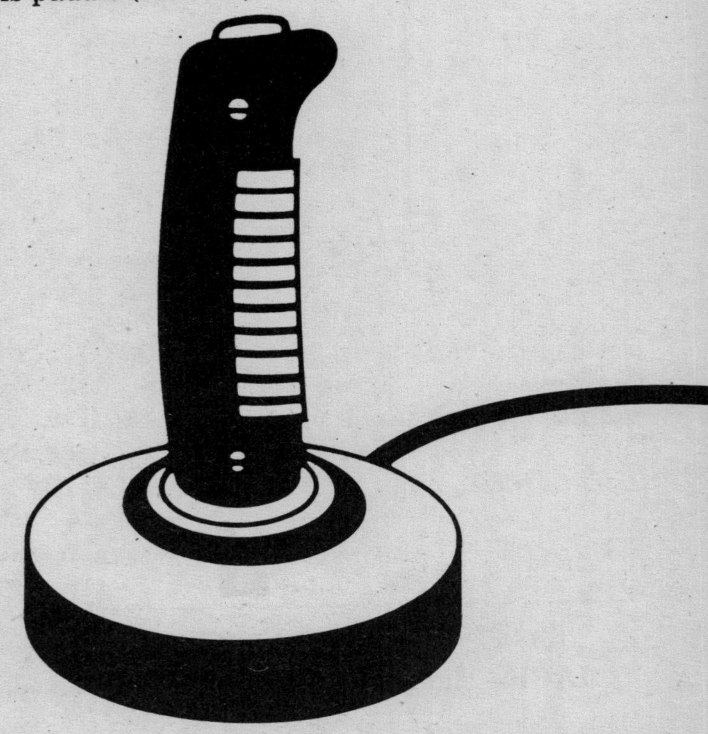

JUSTIFY—To make the left and/or right edges of every line in a paragraph even, one under the other.

K

K—Short for KILO or "one thousand." It means to multiply the number in front of it by 1,000. For example, a 48K computer means it has room in its memory to store 48,000 bytes of data (see BYTE, DATA, MEMORY).

KEYBOARD—Rows of keys which, when pressed, send input into the computer (see INPUT).

KILO—One thousand (see K).

L

LANGUAGE—Sets of words, numbers, and signs grouped according to special rules. To understand a language, you must learn what the words and rules mean. For example, you understand the English language. The computer only understands machine language (see MACHINE LANGUAGE).

LASER—A very thin light beam often used to read bar codes. For example, lasers read bar codes on groceries (see BAR CODE).

LEN—Short for length. A word in BASIC that tells the computer to count the number of characters in a string (see STRING). For example, if you run this little program, the computer will answer 9.

```
10 A$ = BUBBLEGUM
20 PRINT LEN A$
```

LESS THAN (   )—A relational sign which asks the computer to find out if whatever is in front of the sign is smaller than what's in back of the sign.

LET—A BASIC word that tells the computer to make two things equal. For example:

10 LET A = 4

means that after line 10 when the computer sees A, it thinks it is 4 (see VARIABLE).

LIGHT PEN—A pointed rod on a cable connected to the computer. It tells the computer each place you're pointing to on the screen.

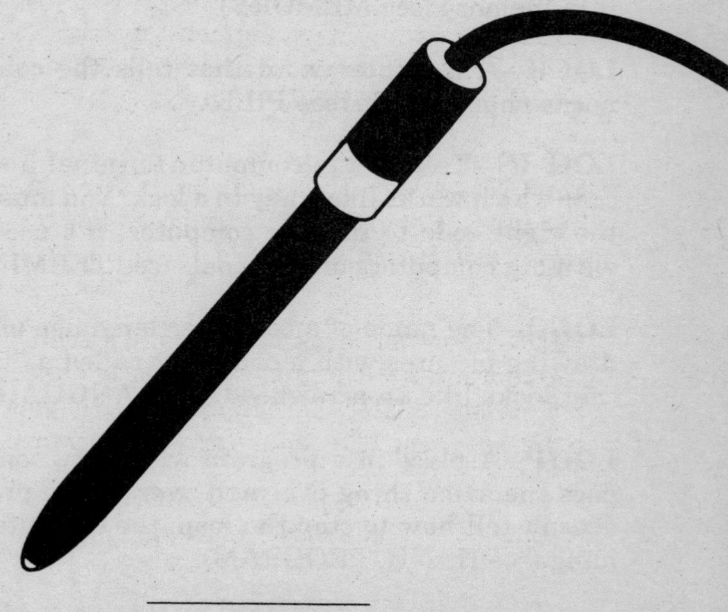

LINE—(1) One instruction in a BASIC program (see INSTRUCTION, PROGRAM); (2) short for telephone line.

LINE NUMBER—The number which must start each line in a BASIC program. The computer uses the line number to do the program in the right order (see PROGRAM).

LIST—A BASIC word that tells the computer to print out the program lines in memory (see MEMORY, PROGRAM).

LOAD—A BASIC word that tells the computer to get a program from a floppy disk or cassette and put it in memory (see MEMORY).

LOCK—A computer word that tells the computer not to change a file (see FILE).

LOG-IN—To give the computer terminal a special code which works like a key in a lock. You must have the right code to use the computer. It's used only with big computers or terminals (see TERMINAL).

LOGO—The name of a computer language used for drawing pictures with a character called a "turtle" that looks like an arrowhead (see LANGUAGE).

LOOP—A place in a program where the computer does the same thing over and over. If the program doesn't tell how to stop the loop, the computer will hang (see HANG, PROGRAM).

M

m—Short for mega or one million. It means to multiply the number in front of it by one million. For example, a 12m memory stores 12,000,000 characters.

MACHINE LANGUAGE—The computer's language. Machine language is the only language the computer can understand directly. Every character is made up of binary numbers. A program written in any other language, such as BASIC, must be turned into machine language by a compiler or interpreter (see BINARY, COMPILER, INTERPRETER).

MAGNETIC DISK/MAGNETIC TAPE—Other words for DISK and TAPE. These are used by a computer to record and play back data (see DISK, TAPE).

MEGA—A prefix meaning one million (see m).

MEMORY—Parts of the computer where data and programs are stored. The computer has many kinds of memories such as ROM, RAM, floppy disks, and buffers (see DATA, PROGRAM, MEMORY, ROM, RAM, DISK, BUFFER).

MENU—A list of things a program can do. After seeing a program menu, you can choose one of those things that you want the computer to do (see PROGRAM).

MICRO—Prefix meaning one-millionth or very, very small. For example, a microsecond is one-millionth of a second. The sign for micro is (   ).

MICROCOMPUTER—A very small computer, about the size of a typewriter.

MICROPROCESSOR—A large IC inside the computer. It has the arithmetic unit, CPU, and special ROM and RAM memories. The microprocessor tells the other parts of the computer what to do, and when to do it (see ARITHMETIC UNIT, RAM, ROM, IC).

MILLI—A prefix meaning one-thousandth. For example, a millisecond is one-thousandth of a second.

MINICOMPUTER—A small computer about the size of a washing machine. It was invented before the microcomputer and is faster, more expensive, and has more memory than a microcomputer.

MODEM—Short for **MO**dulator/**DEM**odulator. It is the interface used to connect a computer to a telephone line (see INTERFACE).

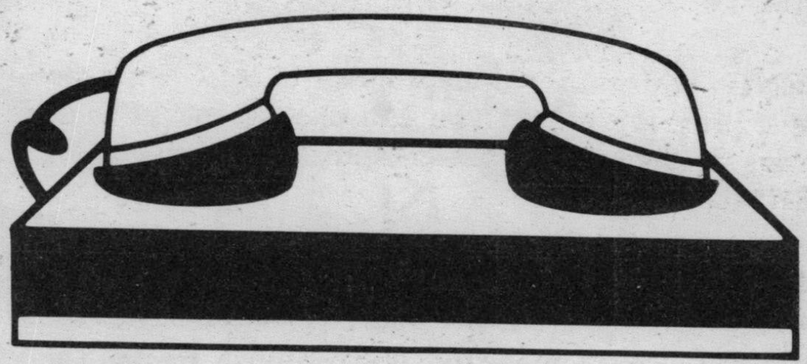

MONITOR—A video screen connected to a computer. It's one place where the computer prints out data. It looks like a TV set without a channel selector.

N

NANO—Prefix meaning one-billionth or one-thousandth of a millionth. For example, a nanosecond is one-billionth of a second—a very, very, short time.

NETWORK—Computers and terminals connected together by modems and telephone lines are called a computer network (see MODEM and TERMINAL).

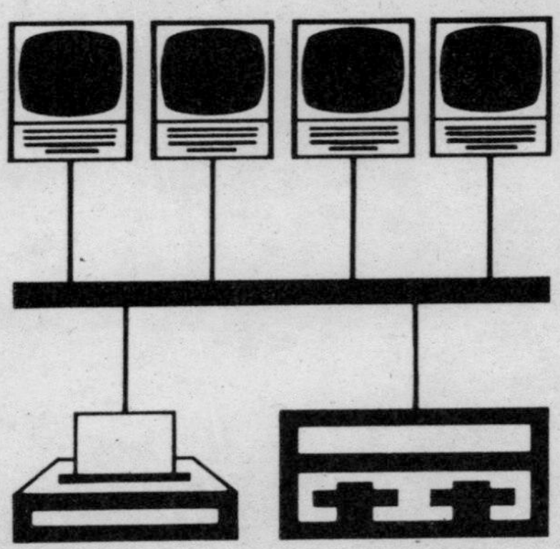

NEW—A word in BASIC that tells the computer to get ready for a new program and to erase the program in memory. Be sure you want to erase a program before pressing RETURN after typing NEW (see MEMORY).

NEXT—The word in a "FOR. . .NEXT" statement that tells the computer when to go round the loop again. For example, this little program:

```
10  FOR N= 1 to 3
20  PRINT N
30  NEXT N
```

tells the computer first to take the number 1, print it, next go back to the FOR statement and get the next number 2, print it, next to go back to the FOR statement and get the next number, 3 and print that.

NIBBLE—Half a byte or 4 binary bits. For example, 1001 is a nibble. Two nibbles make a byte. 1001 1001 is a byte and, in machine language, stands for the letter Y (see BIT, BYTE, MACHINE LANGUAGE).

O

OFF–LINE—A word meaning that a computer interface is disconnected from its line and cannot receive or send data. For example, if a printer is off-line, it cannot receive data from a computer. It's the opposite of on-line (see ON-LINE, DATA, INTERFACE).

ON–LINE—A word meaning that a computer interface is connected to its line and can receive and send data. It's the opposite of off-line (see OFF-LINE, DATA, INTERFACE).

OPERATOR—(1) The name for the "what-to-do" arithmetic signs like plus (+), minus (–), multiply (*), and divide (/); (2) a person who uses a computer.

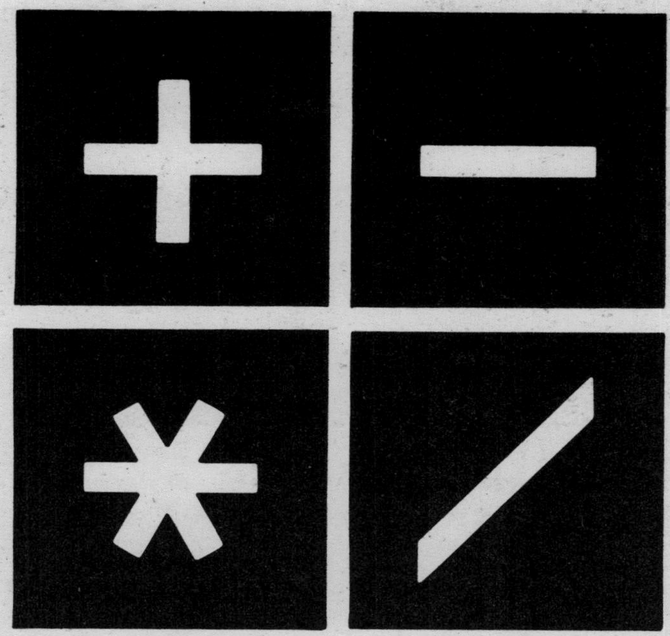

OPTICAL SCANNER—A machine that uses light beams, usually lasers, to read bar code labels. For example, many grocery store checkouts have optical scanners connected to their computers to read bar code labels on products and run the cash register (see LASER, BAR CODE).

OR—A word in BASIC meaning the same as it does in English. It's used only in "IF. . .THEN" statements. For example: 10 IF A=2 or 5 or 7 THEN GOTO 160

OUTPUT—Data sent out by a computer. For example, words sent out to a screen or printer are called output (see OUTPUT).

P

PADDLE—A control such as a knob or stick mounted on a box connected to the computer by a cable. When you turn the knob or move the stick, it sends signals through the cable to the computer. Another name for paddle is joystick (see CABLE, JOYSTICK).

PARENTHESES ( )—Used in arithmetic statements to group operations. They tell the computer to do the operations inside the parentheses first. For example, in this statement, the parentheses tell the computer to add before multiplying (see OPERATOR).

A=3 * (4+2)

PASCAL—The name of a computer language. It was named for the famous French mathematician and scientist Blaise Pascal (1623–1662). (See LANGUAGE.)

PASSWORD—A special code word the user must input before the computer will do anything more (see CODE, INPUT).

PC BOARD—Short for printed circuit board. It's a thin plastic sheet that holds ICs and connects them and other small electrical parts together (see IC).

PEEK—A word in BASIC that tells the computer to look at a memory address and tell you what is stored there. It's the opposite of POKE (see ADDRESS, MEMORY, POKE).

PERCENT (%)—A sign on the keyboard usually used as a prompt (see PROMPT).

PERIOD—A language sign on the keyboard.

PERIPHERAL—A piece of equipment which works with the computer. For example, a printer or disk drive is a peripheral.

PILOT—Name for a computer language (see LANGUAGE).

PLOT—A word in BASIC which lights one square on the screen. For example,

10 PLOT 5,20

will light a square 5 places to the right and 20 places down on the screen from the Home position.

PLOTTER—A computer peripheral which draws pictures on paper. Some plotters can draw in several colors (see PERIPHERAL).

PLUS (+)—A math sign on the keyboard which tells the computer to add two numbers (see OPERATOR).

POKE—A word in BASIC that tells the computer to put a number or letter at an address. It's the opposite of PEEK (see ADDRESS, PEEK).

PORT—The place inside a computer where peripherals are connected. For example, the printer is often connected to the computer's port #1 (see PERIPHERAL).

PRINT—A BASIC word that tells the computer to write on the screen or printer.

PRINTOUT—Computer output printed on paper. This is also called hard copy (see HARD COPY, OUTPUT).

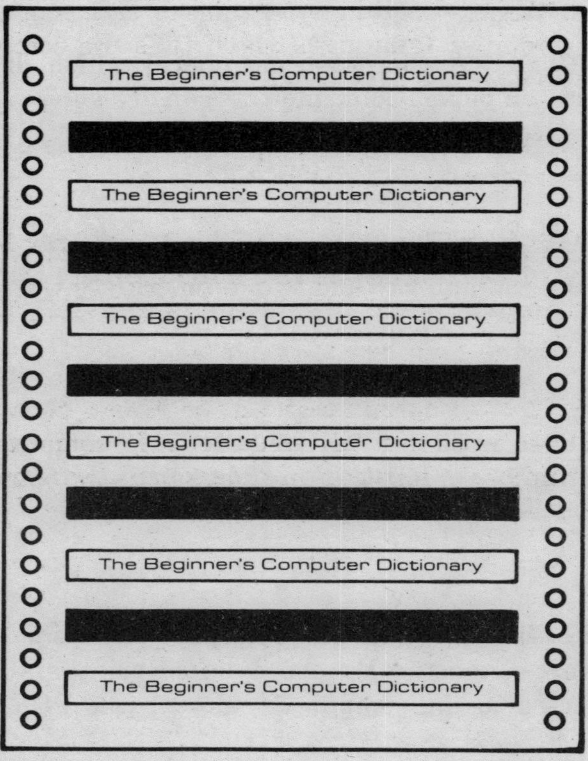

PRINTER—A machine connected to a computer that prints on paper and makes printouts or hard copy (see HARD COPY, PRINTOUT).

PROCESSING—The work the computer does to follow the instructions in a program and produce output (see INSTRUCTION, OUTPUT, PROGRAM).

PROGRAM—List of instructions or orders, written in a computer language, which tells the computer what to do (see LANGUAGE).

PROGRAMMER—The person who writes a computer program (see PROGRAM).

PROM—Short for Programmable Read Only Memory. A PROM works just like a ROM except that the user can put the data into ROM (see DATA, MEMORY, ROM, USER).

PROMPT—A special sign on the screen or printer which tells you that the computer is ready for input. For example, a question mark is sometimes used as a prompt (see INPUT).

Q

QUESTION MARK (?)—A sign in BASIC used as a prompt. It asks for input from the keyboard (see INPUT, KEYBOARD, PROMPT).

QUOTATION MARKS (" ")—Signs used in pairs to tell the computer what to print on the screen or printer. The computer prints exactly what is between the two sets of marks.

QWERTY—Used as a nickname for the computer keyboard. You can easily print QWERTY by pressing the first 6 alphabet keys in the second row (see KEYBOARD).

R

RAM—Short for Random Access Memory. This is the computer's working memory, where data and programs are stored. Anything stored in RAM can be found and changed quickly. On most computers, everything in RAM is erased when the power is turned off (see ACCESS TIME, DATA, MEMORY, PROGRAM).

READ—A computer word that means "get data from memory." When a computer reads, it gets data from its disk, tape, or RAM. READ is also a BASIC word that tells the computer to get data from a data list in a program (see DATA, MEMORY, DISK, RAM, TAPE, WRITE).

READY—A word the computer puts on the screen telling the user that it's ready to work.

REGISTER—A very small memory in the CPU.

Registers can handle only one or two bytes of data. They work at high speed (see ACCUMULATOR, BYTE, DATA).

RELATIONAL SIGNS (=,<,>,< >)—Signs which tell the computer to compare two things. For example, in the program line:

10 IF A < 2 THEN GOTO 50

This tells the computer to compare the value of A with 2 and if the value of A is less than 2, goto line 50 (see PROGRAM).

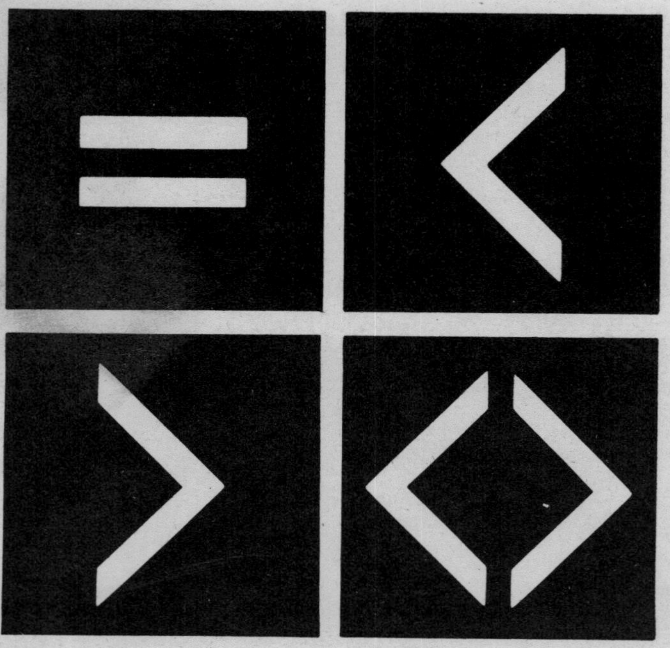

REM—Short for REMARK. A word in BASIC that lets you make remarks to help you remember how a program works. The computer pays no attention to REM statements when the program is run. REM statements are only printed by the computer when it's asked to list a program (see LIST, PROGRAM, RUN, STATEMENT).

REPEAT—The name of a key which tells the computer to print the last key pressed again. Sometimes it is spelled RPT.

RESET—A special and powerful key which sets up all parts of the computer to make a new start. It's powerful because if you press it by mistake, it may erase the program you have in memory (see ERASE, MEMORY, PROGRAM).

RESTORE—A word in BASIC that tells the computer to start reading a data list again from the beginning (see DATA).

RETURN—(1) The name of a key which tells the computer that it's okay to read your message. When you've finished typing, press the RETURN key to send your message into the computer; (2) a word in BASIC that is the second part of a GOSUB. . .RETURN statement. It tells the computer to go back to where it started (see GOSUB).

RND—Short for **R**a**ND**om number. RND is a word in BASIC that tells the computer to choose a number. You never know what number you will get; it's a surprise. That's what random means.

ROM—Short for Read Only Memory. A ROM is a memory chip with data on it which is put on at the factory. The data on ROM chips can never be changed. ROM chips are used in computers and in other places, such as printers and disk drives (see DATA, CHIP, MEMORY).

RUN—A word in BASIC that tells the computer to go to work on the program (see PROGRAM).

S

SAVE—A word in BASIC that tells the computer to put a program on a disk or cassette (see CASSETTE, DISK, PROGRAM).

SCREEN—Short for video screen. This is the place where the computer outputs data to the user (see DATA, USER).

SCROLL—To move lines of words up or down on the screen.

SEMICOLON (;)—A BASIC punctuation mark that tells the computer to print the output close together. For example, if you tell the computer:

```
10 PRINT "ONE";"TWO";"THREE"
```

the computer will print: ONETWOTHREE (see OUTPUT).

SHIFT—The special key which, when pressed with another key, tells the computer to print the top sign on the key.

SILICON—A material for electronic parts made from very pure sand.

SILICON CHIP—A thin, flat piece of silicon made by melting sand and other chemicals. When this material is hardened, it's cut into very thin pieces.

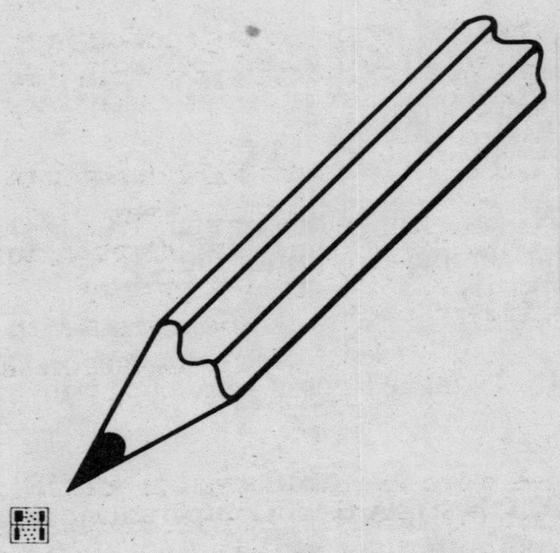

SIMULATION—Computer simulation is a model of a real situation. For example, most computer games are simulations of an adventure.

SLASH—A sign on the keyboard that tells the computer to divide. For example, if you type PRINT 8/2 and press RETURN, the computer will print: 4.

SOFTWARE—Name for all the programs written for the computer (see PROGRAM).

SPACE BAR—A long, unmarked key on the bottom of the keyboard which tells the computer to move ahead each time it's pressed. It prints an empty space.

STATEMENT—A single instruction in a program. For example, here is a program with 3 statements (see PROGRAM):

10 GR	(tells the computer to draw pictures)
20 COLOR=3	(tells the computer to use the color purple)
30 PLOT 15,15	(tells the computer to light up one box on the screen)

STEP—A word in BASIC used in a FOR. . .NEXT LOOP (see FOR, NEXT, LOOP). For example:

40 FOR N= 1 TO 10 STEP2 (tells the computer to count by 2)
50 PRINT N
60 NEXT N
RUN (the computer will print 1,3,5,7,9)

STRING—A line of characters such as letters, blanks, numerals, or signs. The string sign on a keyboard looks like this ($). For example,

A$= "July 4, 1776"

means that the string named A$ is a line of characters meaning July 4, 1776.

SUBROUTINE—A little program which is part of a big program (see GOSUB, PROGRAM).

SYNTAX—Rules for languages. Language rules tell the user how to put numbers, letters, signs, and words together so someone can understand the language. Each computer language like BASIC has its own syntax (see LANGUAGE, USER).

SYNTAX ERROR—The words the computer prints on the screen when it doesn't understand what you've typed. It says you have broken a language rule and you must fix it before the computer can understand you (see LANGUAGE, SYNTAX).

SYSTEM—All the computer hardware and software that work together. For example, the computer, monitor, disk drive, printer, and program disks make up a computer system (see HARDWARE, SOFTWARE, MONITOR, DISK DRIVE, PROGRAM).

T

TAB—A word in BASIC that tells the computer to move the cursor to the right. TAB must be used with the BASIC word PRINT (see CURSOR, PRINT). For example:

```
20 PRINT TAB(10) "DOG"
```

will print the word DOG 10 spaces to the right.

TAPE—Short for MAGNETIC TAPE. A coated plastic ribbon which stores data (see DATA).

TERMINAL—A piece of equipment that looks like a typewriter or a microcomputer. It is usually connected to a computer through a telephone line. It sends and receives data (see MODEM).

TEXT—(1) Computer data that is only letters, numerals or signs—no pictures (see DATA); (2) a word in BASIC that tells the computer to use the screen for words, not for pictures.

TRACTOR—A part of the printer that pulls the paper with the holes in the edge through the printer.

TRANSISTOR—A tiny part that controls the flow of electricity. A chip has thousands of transistors on it. The invention of the transistor in 1951 made it possible to make very small computers (see CHIP, UNIVAC).

TUBE—Short for vacuum tube.

U

UNIVAC—The first electronic computer sold. It used vacuum tubes and was very big (see VACUUM TUBE).

UNLOCK—A computer word that tells the computer it's okay to change a file (see FILE).

USER—The person who works with a computer. Groups of users meet in computer clubs.

V

VACUUM TUBE—An electronic part that controlled the flow of electricity in the first computers. Vacuum tubes are not used in computers now. Smaller electronic parts called transistors do the same job that tubes used to do (see TRANSISTOR).

VARIABLE—The name for a letter which is used like a number. The letter can mean any number you give it.

For example, if you tell the computer:

A = 2

the computer sees A and thinks 2;
If you tell the computer:

A = 4

the computer sees A and thinks 4.

VLIN—A word in Basic which tells the computer to draw a vertical or up-and-down line on the screen. For example, this program line

20 VLIN 1,20 at 5

will draw an up-and-down line on the screen from line 1 to 20 at 5 places across.

VOICE SYNTHESIZER—A computer program which changes output into human voice-like sounds (see PROGRAM, OUTPUT).

W

WAND—A pointed rod attached to the computer by a cable. When the wand is moved across a bar code, it reads the bar code and sends data to the computer (see BAR CODE, CABLE, DATA).

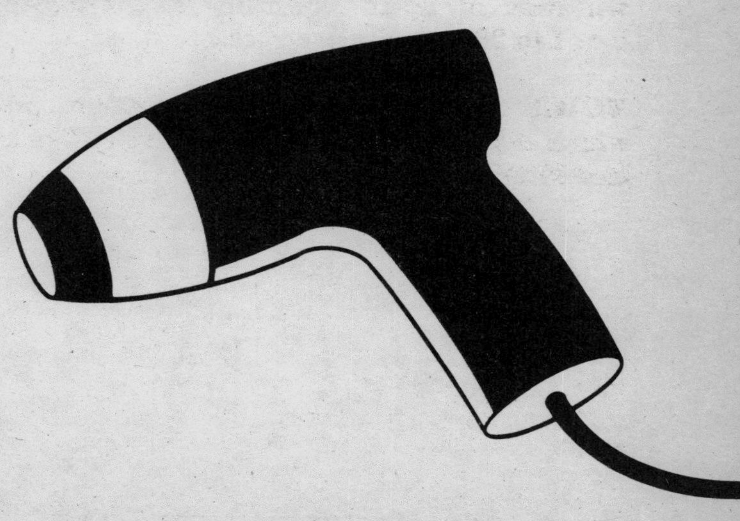

WINCHESTER—A name for a family of hard disks (see HARD DISK).

WORD—In computer language, a WORD is a group of bits (0's and 1's). Most home and school computers have 8-bit words such as 10010001, which is ASCII for Q (see ASCII).

WORD PROCESSING—A way of using the computer to write, change, store, and move words, sentences, and paragraphs quickly and accurately before they are printed on paper.

WRITE—A computer word that means "put data in memory." When the computer WRITES, it saves words and numbers on its disk, tape, or RAM (see DATA, DISK, TAPE, RAM).

X-Y PLOTTER—A machine connected to a computer which can draw lines and pictures on a sheet of paper.

Z

ZERO—A very important part of the computer's machine language. Zero and one are all the computer uses to make its own machine language code for our numbers and alphabet (see MACHINE LANGUAGE, CODE).